T0349707

A World Without Words

compiled by Jasper Morrison

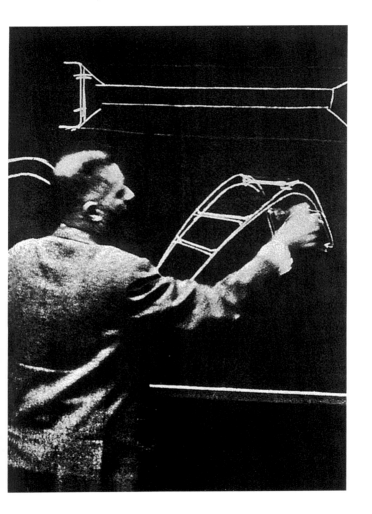

Jean Prouvé

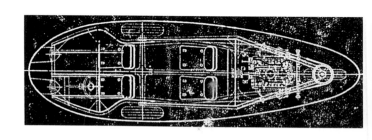

Buckminster Fuller, Dymaxion car

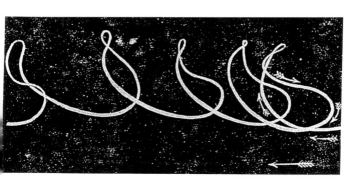

Movement in the tip of a birds wing

Marcos de Celis, Matador

Gerald Summers, one piece plywood chair

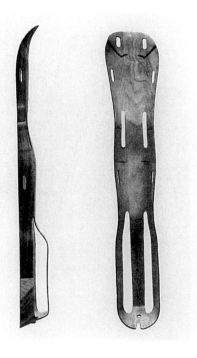

Charles and Ray Eames, leg splint

Fishermens huts, Hastings

Buckminster Fuller, Dymaxion house

Indian Sculpture

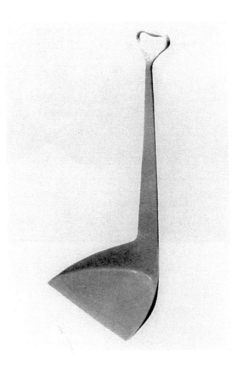

Gino Colombini, plastic dustpan

Coach handle

Atomium, Brussels

Carlo Mollino photograph

Guiseppe Terragni, Como

American grain silos

MERSEY TUNNEL JUNCTION CHAMBER, SHOWING MAIN AND BRANCH TUNNEL. G-1131

Mersey tunnel, Liverpool

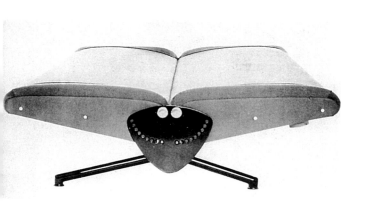

Osvaldo Borsani, sofa/bed

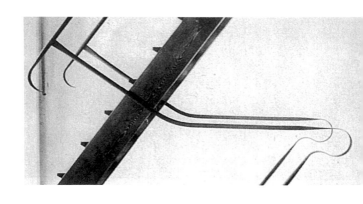

Franco Albini, drop-down staircase

Peter Behrens, Turbine hall, Berlin

Jean Prouvé, folding chair

Achille & Pier Giacomo Castiglioni, tractor seat chair

Tube bending process

Gastone Rinaldi, dual-purpose chair

Cecil Witty, Troy Sunshade Co. USA

Carl Auböck, log table

Graham Bell, 3-way space grid

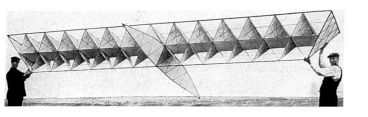

Graham Bell, experimental model of kite plane

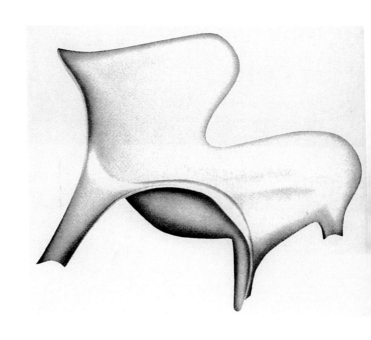

Robert Lewis & James Prestini, moulded plastic chair

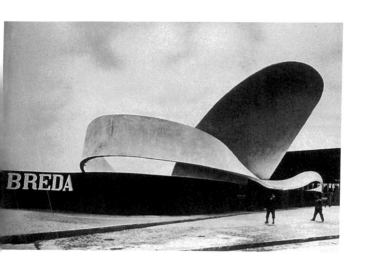

Luciano Baldessari, trade fair pavilion

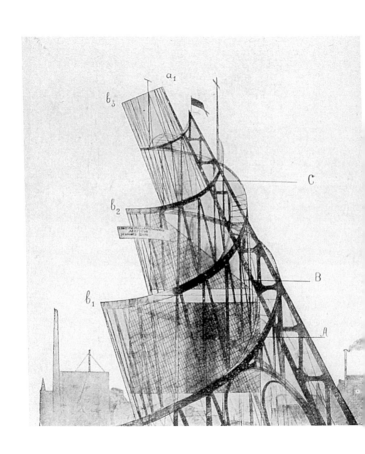

Tatlin's Tower

Yves Klein, Anthropometric painting

Goan house chair

Alvar Aalto, stacking chairs

Buckminster Fuller

Indoor tennis court, Paris

Giacomo Mattè-Trucco, Fiat factory "Lingotto"

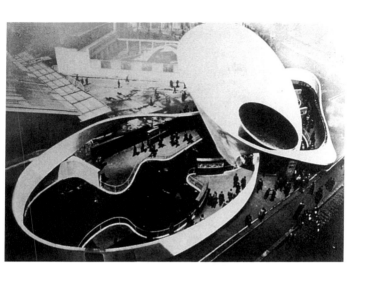

Luciano Baldessari, plan view of trade fair pavilion

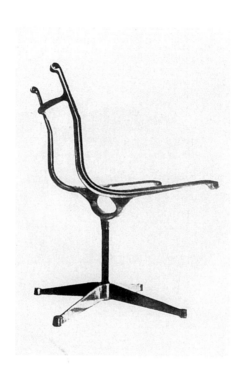

Charles Eames, office chair frame

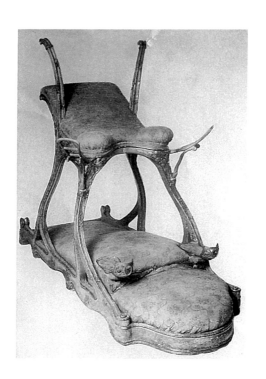

"Fauteuil d'amour"

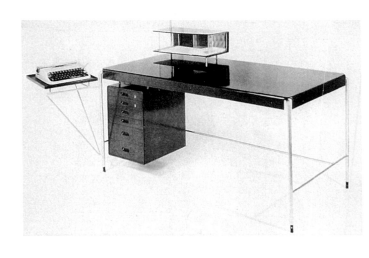

Arne Jacobsen, office desk

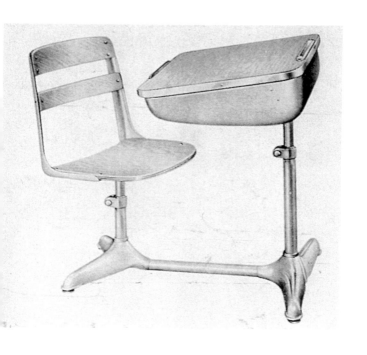

American Seating Co. Grand Rapids, school desk

Triodetic connector

Indian tree protection system

Fiat "Lingotto" test track

Piaggio factory

3 wine bottles

Rome central station

Heinz & Bodo Rasch, "Chair of sitting ghost"

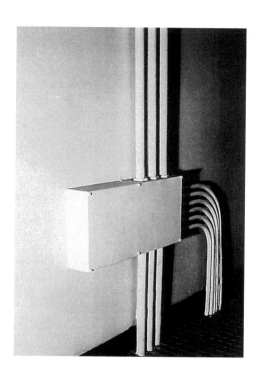

Pierre Chareau, electrical conduit detail, Maison de Verre

Raincoat salesmanship

Gispen's factory demonstration

Gerrit Rietveld, pressed aluminium chair

Radcliffe observatory, Oxford

Guiseppe Terragni, draughtsman's lamp

BBPR, Project for an ideal house

Enzo Mari, self build cupboard

W. Ernst Haas & Son, kitchen cupboard

Ernö Goldfinger, Air France ticket office interior

San Siro stadium, Milan

New York

La Scala, Milan

German Railways door handles

Albert Melniker's house

Railway signals

Prime Minister of Tamil Nadu

Piazza Duomo, Milan

Barcelona Airport

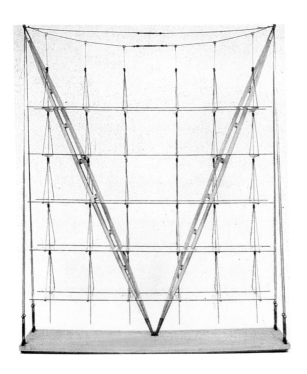

Franco Albini, shelves

Indian tribals, Madhya Pradesh

Gabriele D'Annunzio's boat, Lago di Garda

Italian Railways coach

Danish Postman

Italian sugar packet

Salvador & Gala Dalí, Gala's Salon (which is egg shaped)

Enzo Mari, light-weight stacking chair

Mussolini's EUR, Rome

Emil Fahrenkamp, Shell-Haus, Berlin

Montmatre steps, Paris

Viennese fire hydrant

Guiseppe Terragni, studio interior

Pierre Chareau, house for Robert Motherwell

Technical demonstration of plywood

Jean Prouvé, table base

Anonymous multiple portrait

Thonet, Chair N° 14

Piero Manzoni

Piaggio scooter

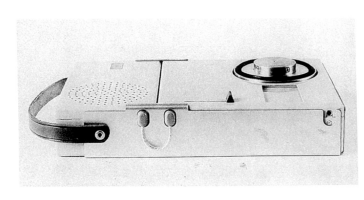

Dieter Rams, portable record player

Takis, Indicators with purple light

Guiseppe Terragni, Como

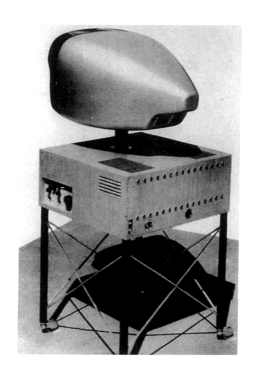

Berizzi, Butte & Montagni, television set

Renzo Zavanella, work station

Luciano Baldessari, architectural model

Photographic studies of French footballers

Circus act

Gio Ponti, Pirelli Building, Milan

Frank Lloyd Wright, Guggenheim Museum

Enzo Mari, self assembly "Box chair"

Jean Prouvé, "Anthony"

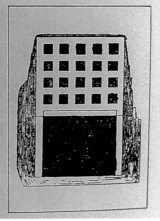

Adolf Loos' inspiration

1st Edition & Graphic Design: Anthony Arefin, London 1992

Printing and binding: Belvédère Art Books, Oosterbeek, the Netherlands
Paper: LuxoArt Silk, 170 g/m^2

©1998/2023 Jasper Morrison
www.jaspermorrison.com

Published by Lars Müller Publishers
Zurich/Switzerland
www.lars-mueller-publishers.com

ISBN 978-3-03778-207-1
Printed in the Netherlands